I0554680

# SELF-LOVE
## Project

**Hanna Olivas & Adriana Luna Carlos**
Along with 9 Inspiring Women

ISBN: 978-1-960136-12-1

# Table of Contents

# INTRODUCTION

She Rises Studios was created and inspired by the mother-daughter duo Hanna Olivas and Adriana Luna Carlos. In the middle of 2020, when the world was at one of its most vulnerable times, we saw the need to embrace women globally by offering inspirational quotes, blogs, and articles. Then, in March of 2021, we launched our very own Women's Empowerment Podcast: *She Rises Studios Podcast*.

It is now one of the most sought out Women based podcasts both nationally and internationally. You can find us on your favorite podcast platforms, such as Spotify, Google Podcasts, Apple Podcasts, IHeartRadio, and much more! We didn't stop there. Establishing a safe space for women has become an even deeper need. Due to a global pandemic, women lost their businesses, employment, homes, finances, spouses, and more.

We decided to form the She Rises Studios Community Facebook Group. An environment strictly for women about women. Our focus in this group is to educate and celebrate women globally. To meet them exactly where they are on their journey.

It's a group of Ordinary Women Doing EXTRAordinary Things.

As we continued to grow our network, we saw a need to help shape the minds and influences of women struggling with insecurities, doubts, fears, etc. From this, we created a global movement known as:

**Self-Love Project**

*Transform your life with Self-Love*

Self-Love Project is a transformative guide to help readers cultivate a deep and genuine sense of self-love.

In this empowering book, readers will embark on a journey of self-discovery, learning practical tools and exercises to overcome self-doubt, negative self-talk, and other limiting beliefs that prevent them from living their best life. With compassion and insight, the author shares personal stories and insights that will inspire readers to embrace their imperfections, set healthy boundaries, and practice self-care.

Drawing on mindfulness, positive psychology, and cognitive-behavioral therapy, this book offers a comprehensive approach to self-love that is both practical and profound. From learning to quiet the inner critic to developing a growth mindset, Self-Love Project offers a roadmap to help readers build a more loving and fulfilling relationship with themselves.

Whether you are looking to boost your confidence, heal from past traumas, or simply live a happier, more authentic life, this book will guide you towards greater self-awareness, self-acceptance, and self-love.

**She Rises Studios offers:**

- She Rises Studios Publishing
- She Rises Studios Public Relations
- She Rises Studios Podcast
- She Rises Studios Magazine
- Becoming An Unstoppable Woman TV Show
- She Rises Studios Community
- She Rises Studios Academy
- KNOWN SRS
- FENIX TV

We won't stop encouraging women to be Unstoppable. This is just the beginning of our global movement.

**She Rises, She Leads, She Lives...**

With Love,
HANNA OLIVAS
ADRIANA LUNA CARLOS
SHE RISES STUDIOS
www.sherisesstudios.com

**Adriana Luna Carlos**

Founder and CEO of She Rises Studios & FENIX TV

https://www.linkedin.com/in/adriana-luna-carlos/
https://www.facebook.com/adrianalunacarlos
https://www.instagram.com/sherisesstudios/
https://www.sherisesstudios.com/
https://www.srslatina.com/
https://fenixtv.app/

Adriana Luna Carlos is an accomplished web and graphic designer, author, and mentor with a passion for helping women succeed in life and business. With over 10 years of experience in graphic and web arts, Adriana has built a reputation as an innovative leader and entrepreneur. In 2020, she co-founded She Rises Studios, a multi-digital media company and publishing house that has helped countless clients achieve their branding and marketing goals. In 2023, she co-created FENIX TV, an online streaming platform that showcases stories of people breaking barriers, shattering stereotypes, and triumphing against the odds.

As an advocate for women's success, Adriana challenges her clients and mentees to strive for nothing less than excellence. She has a deep understanding of the insecurities and challenges that women often face in the business world and provides the guidance and resources needed to overcome them. Her success as a business leader and entrepreneur has made her a sought-after mentor and speaker at events around the world.

Through her work, Adriana has demonstrated a commitment to creating opportunities for women to succeed in business and life. Her passion for innovation, leadership, and women's empowerment has made her a respected figure in the business community, and her impact will undoubtedly continue to inspire and empower women for years to come.

# LEARNING TO LOVE MYSELF

By Adriana Luna Carlos

"I'm good, how are you?" The words flowed effortlessly from my lips, a well-rehearsed script that echoed through the years. But beneath the surface, a hidden truth lingered, concealed from the world and even from myself. I had become an expert at hiding my inner struggles, convinced that vulnerability was a sign of weakness. It took me countless years to realize that this façade stemmed from how I perceived and valued myself. I am going to walk you through the mind of my younger self so that you can uncover with me my self-love discovery journey.

**Behind the Mask**

The mask of "I'm good" shielded me from prying eyes, an armor to deflect any intrusion into my world of turmoil. I believed it was not my place to open up, to let others witness my vulnerabilities. But little did I know, this self-imposed silence gnawed at my soul, denying me the chance to heal and grow. It took me years to comprehend that the root of it all lay in how I cared for and perceived myself.

Of course, it is not necessary to reveal every fiber of our being to the world with each passing encounter. But when the question arises, it is vital to pause and ponder the reasons behind our chosen response. Why do we answer the way we do? Are we speaking our truth or merely perpetuating the charade? These questions hold the key to unraveling the mystery of our self-love journey.

Within my friend group, I was known as the perpetual apologist—the one who apologized for even the most trivial of matters. Yes, everything warranted my remorse, every action or word. Perhaps, deep down, I yearned for them to understand that I harbored no intention to cause pain, or offense, or allow the faintest glimpse of negativity to taint their perception of me. I was constantly overthinking, my mind filled with doubts about my true identity and whether this was the person I even wanted to be.

Each time, it was my friends who gently reminded me that no apologies were necessary, assuring me that I had done nothing wrong. We would laugh and joke about my habit and make light of it. Yet, as I returned home, the lingering wonder persisted, questioning why breaking this habit seemed so elusive.

**My Turning Point**

In the early days of my twenties, a profound realization washed over me, revealing that the root of it all lay in a scarcity of self-love. It was during this time that a friend asked me to write words of affirmation and recite them aloud. Yet, as I attempted to put pen to paper, laughter bubbled up within me. But this laughter was masking my fear and frustration and helped me to see my struggle to perceive in myself what others saw. Even the simplest words, like "smart," felt unworthy to claim, for they invited doubt to seep into my being, questioning if I truly possessed such qualities.

If I knew anything about myself it was that I was a fighter and I never gave up. I became determined to conquer this unfamiliar territory in my mind. After all, I already had an immense love for psychology and understanding people's psyches. It was time to learn about myself. I knew it wouldn't be easy but I wanted to understand and love myself.

**Embracing Authenticity**

With each step along this path, I shed the weight of unnecessary apologies. I embraced the imperfections that define our shared human experience, recognizing that they do not diminish my essence but enrich it. The symphony of self-doubt gradually faded, replaced by a newfound melody of self-assurance and genuine connection.

Embracing self-love and authenticity is a transformative journey that requires consistent practice and mindfulness. Start by cultivating self-awareness, tuning into your thoughts and emotions. Notice any doubts or negative self-talk that arises, and challenge them with compassion and kindness. Replace self-doubt with affirmations that reinforce your worth and uniqueness. Surround yourself with positive influences and supportive individuals who uplift and celebrate your true self. Practice self-care rituals that nourish your mind, body, and spirit, such as meditation, exercise, and engaging in activities that bring you joy.

Remember, authenticity is about embracing your genuine self, so allow yourself to express your true thoughts and emotions without fear of judgment. Embrace imperfections as opportunities for growth and learning, celebrating your journey towards self-love.

In my business endeavors, I learned to value my worth and set healthy boundaries. I became more selective with the projects I took on, ensuring they aligned with my values and allowed me to express my true self. I celebrated my achievements and acknowledged that setbacks and failures were part of the journey, not reflections of my worth.

My message to others is simple: You are worthy of love and happiness, exactly as you are. Embrace self-love as a lifelong practice, and remember that it's not selfish or indulgent. By loving and caring for yourself, you cultivate the strength and resilience needed to make a positive impact on the world around you.

As I conclude this chapter, I want to extend my heartfelt gratitude to each and every one of you. Self-love is a transformative journey, and I hope that by sharing my own experiences and insights, I have inspired you to embark on your own path of self-discovery and self-acceptance. Remember, you are enough, and your unique gifts and talents deserve to be celebrated. Embrace the power of self-love, and watch as it radiates into every aspect of your life, filling it with joy, purpose, and fulfillment.

# A Dance with Life's Lessons

*In the tender embrace of each passing day,*
*Life's teachings gracefully come my way.*

*I pause, allowing them to seep into my core,*
*Like a melody, they resonate, forevermore.*

*I seek a song, a sweet harmony of truth,*
*To intertwine with the lessons of my youth.*

*Its notes, a gentle river, caressing my soul,*
*Ensuring the message remains forever whole.*

*For in the depths of emotions, I immerse,*
*Feeling the essence of wisdom, like a verse.*

*I let them guide me, whispering their lore,*
*Etching their wisdom in the fabric of my core.*

*A vow to life, to flourish and grow,*
*From each encounter, my strength does bestow.*

*For the tapestry of existence, woven so vast,*
*Holds treasures for me, a future unsurpassed.*

*So, let us make it our purpose to embrace,*
*The gifts that life presents, in every space.*

*For in the acceptance of what life may bring,*
*Our souls find solace, and our spirits sing.*

*In this symphony of growth, we find our might,*
*Through self-love's embrace, we shine so bright.*

*Each lesson learned, a stepping stone to endure,*
*Transforming us into beings resilient and pure.*

*As we dance with life, hand in hand,*
*Let self-love be our guiding command.*

*For in its tender embrace, we find our worth,*
*A love that nourishes our souls, from birth.*

*So, let us heed life's teachings, one and all,*
*Embracing the rise and the occasional fall.*

*For in the journey, we become whole,*
*United with self-love, our essence of gold.*

*In this lesson to you, I extend my plea,*
*Let the beauty of self-love forever be.*

*May its whispers linger, forever true,*
*Guiding you to a life that's authentically you.*

*—Adriana Luna Carlos*

## Hanna Olivas

Founder & CEO of She Rises Studios
Podcast & TV Host | Best Selling Author | Influential Speaker |
Blood Cancer Advocate | #BAUW Movement Creator

https://www.linkedin.com/company/she-rises-studios/
https://www.facebook.com/sherisesstudios
https://www.instagram.com/sherisesstudios
www.SheRisesStudios.com

Author, Speaker, and Founder. Hanna was born and raised in Las Vegas, Nevada, and has paved her way to becoming one of the most influential women of 2022. Hanna is the co-founder of She Rises Studios and the founder of the Brave & Beautiful Blood Cancer Foundation. Her journey started in 2017 when she was first diagnosed with Multiple Myeloma, an incurable blood cancer. Now more than ever, her focus is to empower other women to become leaders because The Future is Female. She is currently traveling and speaking publicly to women to educate them on entrepreneurship, leadership, and owning the female power within.

# EMBRACING SELF-LOVE: MY JOURNEY OF HEALING FROM TRAUMA

## By Hanna Olivas

In this chapter, I will share my personal journey of finding self-love after years of not valuing myself as I should have. From a young age, I experienced sexual abuse, molestation, and later on, domestic violence. These experiences left me feeling disconnected from love, both from others and within myself. However, through my own healing process, I discovered steps that helped me cultivate true self-love and embrace my uniqueness. In this chapter, I will delve into those steps, offering guidance on how to heal from past trauma, overcome feelings of unworthiness, and live in true self-love at all times.

**The Impact of Trauma:**

As someone who has experienced trauma, I understand the deep and lasting effects it can have on self-perception, self-worth, and the ability to love oneself. The profound impact of sexual abuse, molestation, and domestic violence shaped my view of myself and made self-love feel like a foreign concept. It took time for me to recognize how these experiences had influenced my beliefs and behaviors. Understanding the impact of trauma is crucial to begin the healing journey.

**Acknowledgment and Validation:**

One of the most important steps in my healing process was acknowledging and validating my experiences. For years, I had suppressed my pain and emotions, denying the impact they had on me. But by acknowledging the truth of what I went through and allowing myself to feel the pain, I created a safe space for self-reflection and acceptance. It was a challenging process, but it allowed me to validate my own experiences and recognize that what happened to me was not my fault.

**Seeking Support:**

Healing from trauma should never be done alone. I realized that seeking professional support from therapists or counselors specializing in trauma was crucial to my healing. These professionals provided a safe and non-judgmental space for me to explore my emotions, process my experiences, and gain valuable insights. Additionally, I learned the importance of building a support system of understanding individuals who could provide love and encouragement throughout my journey.

**Reclaiming Personal Power:**

One significant aspect of my healing journey was reclaiming my personal power. I realized that the trauma I experienced did not define my worth or identity. It required a conscious effort to develop resilience, set healthy boundaries, and redefine the narratives I had about myself. Through therapy and self-reflection, I began to recognize my strengths, talents, and inherent worthiness. It was a transformative process that allowed me to regain control over my life and cultivate self-compassion.

**Cultivating Self-Love:**

The concept of self-love was something I struggled with for a long time. But as I began to heal, I learned that self-love goes beyond superficial notions. It involves practicing self-care, accepting myself as I am, and showing compassion towards my own imperfections. Mindfulness became a powerful tool for me, allowing me to stay present, appreciate myself, and practice positive self-talk. Embracing self-expression through various outlets, such as art or writing, also played a vital role in nurturing my self-love.

**Healing from Past Trauma:**

Healing from trauma is a complex and individualized process. I explored various therapeutic techniques and coping mechanisms to promote my healing. Cognitive-behavioral therapy helped me challenge negative thought patterns and develop healthier coping strategies. Somatic therapy allowed me to reconnect with my body and release stored trauma. Engaging in creative outlets, like art or writing, provided me with a means of self-expression and processing my emotions. Each person's healing journey is unique, and it's important to find the techniques that resonate with you.

**Embracing Uniqueness and Finding Belonging:**

Throughout my life, I often felt different and unworthy. However, on my path to self-love, I realized that embracing my uniqueness was essential. I began to celebrate my individuality and find a sense of belonging in communities that accepted and supported me. Surrounding myself with understanding and like-minded individuals played a significant role in my healing journey.

**Breaking the Cycle of Self-Medication:**

Escaping self-judgment and self-shame has been an incredibly difficult journey for me. For so long, I carried the weight of self-criticism and shame, wondering how many other women out there also experienced a lack of self-love. In my attempt to cope, I resorted to self-medication, using it as a way to numb myself and avoid facing my innermost thoughts. However, I soon realized that this only perpetuated the cycle of self-destructive patterns. It has been a challenging process, but I am committed to breaking free from these harmful tendencies and embracing self-love.

**Seeing Myself in a Positive Light:**

When I finally saw myself in a positive light, it was like love at first sight. The moment I recognized my own beauty and the goodness within my heart, I fell in love with who I had become. Each and every day, as I wake up and look in the mirror, I see the reflection of someone I genuinely love and cherish. It has been a long and challenging journey to get to this point, but every step, every tear shed, and every moment of self-discovery has been completely worth it. I am grateful for the growth, the healing, and the transformation that has brought me to this place of self-love.

**My Heart:**

In my heart, I hold a firm belief that every human being deserves to love themselves deeply and wholeheartedly. It is not only a personal journey but also a responsibility to guide and inspire others to embark on their own paths of self-love. When we cultivate a life of love and beauty from within ourselves, it radiates outward, positively impacting every aspect of our existence. I have witnessed firsthand how embracing self-love has transformed my life, and I am passionate about encouraging others to do the same. By nurturing love and acceptance within ourselves, we create a ripple effect, spreading love and beauty to the world around us. It all starts within our hearts, and when we live a life rooted in self-love, everything else falls into place.

**Faith in Myself:**

During my journey of discovering self-love, I came to realize that a significant part of it was having faith in myself, even during moments when I couldn't see, feel, or hear the difference it was making. There were times when doubts and insecurities crept in, making me question if this path of self-love was truly worth it. But deep within, I had an unwavering belief that I deserved love and that cultivating self-love was crucial for my well-being. So, even when progress seemed slow or imperceptible, I remained faithful to my journey. I held onto the belief that with time, patience, and consistent effort, I would experience a transformation that would bring me the self-love and acceptance I longed for.

Throughout the ups and downs, I stayed committed to my path of self-love. It wasn't always easy, and there were moments when I stumbled or felt discouraged. But I refused to give up. I reminded myself that self-love is a lifelong journey, and the results may not always be immediate or tangible. I trusted the process and the small steps I was taking each day, knowing that they were building the foundation for a healthier and more fulfilling life. My faith in myself and the power of self-love fueled my determination, allowing me to persevere through challenges and setbacks. And as I look back now, I am grateful for staying faithful to my journey because it has led me to a place of self-love and empowerment that I never thought possible.

Oftentimes, I found myself tempted to revert to my old ways, to slip back into patterns of self-destruction that I had grown comfortable with. It was as if there was an internal battle between the familiarity of my past and the desire to truly love myself. But I recognized that surrendering to those old patterns would only perpetuate the cycle of self-destruction, and I would have to start the journey of self-love all over again. It was a sobering realization that pushed me to break free from that destructive pattern once and for all. I made a firm commitment to myself to focus on rebuilding my self-love, refusing to let setbacks deter me from my ultimate goal.

Let us shift our focus and dedicate ourselves to rebuilding our self-love once and for all. It's time to break free from the cycle of starting over and make a lasting change. We owe it to ourselves to break the pattern of self-destruction and embrace a path of self-empowerment. By consciously choosing self-love every day, we can rebuild ourselves from the inside out and create a foundation of self-worth and inner strength that will withstand any challenges that come our way. It may not always be easy, but with determination, perseverance, and a steadfast commitment to our own well-being, we can transform our lives and experience the true depth and beauty of self-love.

**Live your life without limits and lots of self-love:**

I have come to realize that living life without limits is intricately tied to embracing self-love. When we truly love ourselves, we break free from the constraints and limitations that society or our own negative self-perceptions may impose upon us. Self-love allows us to acknowledge our worth, strengths, and unique qualities, empowering us to pursue our passions and dreams with unwavering confidence. It is a mindset that encourages us to take risks, step out of our comfort zones, and explore the vast possibilities that life has to offer. By living a life fueled by self-love, we unlock our true potential and open ourselves up to a world of limitless opportunities and fulfillment.

So, let us embark on this journey of self-love, embracing it wholeheartedly and without reservation. Let us break free from the chains of self-doubt and fear, and instead, nurture a deep sense of love and acceptance for ourselves. With self-love as our guiding compass, we can approach every aspect of life with authenticity, compassion, and a sense of freedom. It is through embracing self-love that we cultivate a life filled with joy, fulfillment, and the courage to pursue our passions unapologetically. Let us live each day with a fierce love for ourselves, knowing that we are deserving of a life without limits.

My journey towards self-love was a process of self-discovery, healing, and growth. It required acknowledging the impact of trauma, seeking support, reclaiming personal power, cultivating self-love, and embracing my uniqueness. Although the healing journey is ongoing, I now understand that true self-love is possible, no matter how late it may come in life. By sharing my story and the steps I followed, I hope to inspire and support others on their own paths towards healing and self-love.

## Nicole Curtis

She Rises Studios
Co-Founder of the Women Leadership Division

https://www.linkedin.com/in/nicole-curtis-sherisesstudios
https://www.facebook.com/nicolecurtissherisesstudios
https://www.instagram.com/nicolecurtis_sherisesstudios/
https://www.sherisesstudios.com/
https://www.facebook.com/groups/sherisesstudioscommunity

Speaker, 9x International Best Selling Author and Co-Founder. Nicole Curtis was born and raised in Holland, MI and is a much sought-after leader in women's Personal Growth and Self-Leadership Development. Nicole is the Co-Founder of the She Rises Studios Women Leadership Division. She teaches, mentors and leads women around the world how to master the art of self-leadership so that they can Rise, Lead and Live in life and in business.

# SELF-LOVE FOR THE SOUL 🖤

By Nicole Curtis

I spent much of my life pouring as much love into other people as I could because I believed this was how you love yourself, but over the years, it only made me hate myself. I was so busy loving everyone else that the "leftover love" I felt came from a place of exhaustion, brokenness, and disgrace. I hated my reflection in the mirror. I never had anything nice to say to myself, and I treated my mind and soul literally like scrapes. I was so wrapped up in perfecting my exterior love that I abandoned my self-love.

The lack of love I had was due to all the ugliness and resentment I felt about myself. I believed the only love I could have would come from other people because I wasn't capable or worthy enough to love myself until just a few years ago. I was on my bedroom floor on my knees in front of my mirror, screaming and ugly crying into my pillow. I was sick of how things were going in life, and one of them was how I felt about myself. As I looked up and stared into the mirror, I was horrified by how empty the face staring back at me looked. All I saw was a lost, lonely, ugly, worthless woman who had no respect, value, or appreciation, let alone any love for herself.

I was tired of feeling this way, so in that moment, I chose to listen to the voice inside of me that was saying, "God doesn't make junk he makes diamonds, so start sparkling Nicole." This was the first time I felt a small glimpse of hope, and oddly enough, peace filled my heart. I then had to decide whether to continue on the path I was on or change. I wanted change so badly, but I was afraid to. I didn't believe I was worthy enough of it, so I told myself I would commit to this change thing for ninety days. For ninety days, I was going to strive to better myself, and the first thing I was going to start learning was how to replace all the cold feelings and thoughts I had about myself and start replacing them with loving ones. This started my self-love for the soul journey, and let me tell you, it wasn't easy. But I am so proud that I chose myself and decided that I was worth it.

Over the years, I have learned and implemented a lot of strategies centered around self-love. There is so much out there, but what has worked the best for me is a self-love process that I actually created on my own, and I want to share it with you. I want you, too, to feel what real love really feels like and help you become a sparkling, soul-loving woman who loves herself wholeheartedly.

The Self-Love For The Soul 💜 Process:

**1. The power to choose!**

Change can only start with you, nobody else!

**2. Decide that it is going to happen and then start!**

In order for steps 1 & 2 to work, you really need to dive deep within yourself and get honest, raw, and real with yourself. Explore where you are at in life emotionally and mentally, then establish what you want to see change, and lastly, list the reasons why. This will give you your starting point!

**3. Free yourself**

Love yourself wholeheartedly! The goal here is for you to love yourself with a sense of wholeness, peace, and empowerment. Examine the beliefs about your life and yourself and then challenge these beliefs to see if they are truly beneficial to your health and happiness. Areas to focus on here are people pleasing, imperfections, self-doubt, and compassionate thinking ( in any given moment, you're either judging yourself or accepting yourself).

A few ways to help you love yourself wholeheartedly is through journaling. Take five minutes (or longer, if you have the time) to journal. Doing this creates a space for you to write everything out. Write out what you are feeling and thinking. Example: What do you fear/ what excites you. This helps you get it out of your head and heart to see a clearer picture. Doing this exercise helps you become honest with your feelings and thoughts so that you can begin to adjust what you want to see changed.

The second way is to follow your heart. Become the woman you want to be and do the things that you want to do. There is nothing wrong with following what makes you happy or doing the things that bring you peace.

The last one is self-forgiveness. This one was a biggie for me because, as I mentioned previously, I carried around a lot of ugliness and resentment that led me to hate myself. Having self-forgiveness literally saved me. In order to move forward in my self-love journey, I had to forgive myself for all the hurt and hate I put myself through. I had to wash away the ugly talk, actions, and thoughts about myself to make room for clarity, understanding, self-respect, trust, self-worth, and appreciation. Self-forgiveness literally took me from the darkness and showed me how to sparkle with self-love.

One of the exercises I did, which I still do to this day, is to take out a notepad and pen and write down everything that you are thinking and feeling that is negative about yourself. In doing this, it doesn't matter if it is one word, five words, or 50 words. The point is to get all the crap thinking and thoughts out on paper. Once you are done, I want you to replace all of the nasty words/ statements with a positive, loving, and uplifting word/statement on a separate piece of paper. Example: *I am not good enough* is replaced with *I am not feeling good enough now, but I will feel it soon because I am working hard at loving myself more each day*. It takes time, but trust the process. I will never give up because I am worthy too. Once you have replaced all the nasty with good, then I want you to take the nasty list and either rip it up or (what I like to do) burn it.

When doing this, you will feel so empowered and renewed because you are letting go of all that nastiness. I urge you to try this exercise and see just how freeing it really is, and if you want to share your experience with me, I would love to hear all about it. Send me a DM on one of my socials—links are listed before my chapter bio.

**4. Unapologetic Love**

When you accept and love all of yourself (the good, the bad, and the messy), remarkable things happen! Validation and approval from others were so important to me at one point. I constantly tried so hard to be like everyone else, and I would always compare myself to them. I didn't accept myself for who I was, hence another example of "leftover love." I wanted to be someone else because I thought this, too, was a way to love myself.

I had to work the hardest at unapologetic love, which is why it is so important to me to lead my life with it! I struggled because I had to completely rewire my mindset. In doing so, I was able to create and get rid of a lot of yuck that I thought and felt about myself over the years. Unapologetic love has helped me realize my qualities, and ease my feelings of guilt and shame along with my self-sabotaging thoughts. A key point of unapologetic love is to be kind to yourself. Love yourself no matter what, whether the day is good or bad, and always accept your imperfections! God doesn't make junk, he makes diamonds, so go sparkle bright!

**5. Control Your Mind**

Our minds control our consciousness, and our consciousness allows us to acknowledge our personal character, feelings, motives, and desires. This means your focus needs to be on your mind, heart, and soul. One way to do this is by having self-awareness. Self-awareness helps empower you to make changes so that you can build up your strengths and helps you identify areas where you need improvement. In this, you are able to not only see what you are good at but what are some things you can improve in or areas you can grow in.

The benefits of this help you improve skills and recognize what you do well but also what you can improve on. It also helps raise your happiness levels by aligning your ideals with your actions. Example regarding my motives and desires: what do I want to create or where do I want to be as a woman in my self-love journey six months, a year, or even five years from now?

Another benefit of self-awareness is that you become more in tune with your emotions, which helps manage them. When you acknowledge your personal character or feelings, it allows you to then take a step back and ask yourself questions like "How am I doing," " How am I feeling," and " Why do I feel this way?" Doing this helps you gauge your levels of emotions which actually diminishes your own feelings/beliefs from others and opens the door to actually asking yourself questions. This was really hard for me in the beginning because I wasn't used to asking myself any kind of questions in my life, like what do I want, what do I believe, or what is true in my heart.

Practicing self-awareness helps ignite and grow your self-love because it gives you the ability to ask yourself questions which is freeing and aligning because the more you do this, the more you actually get to know yourself, and the more you do this, the more you love yourself because you are valuing and honoring yourself on a whole new level. Become your own best friend!

**6. Give Yourself Permission to Love Yourself First**

As a woman leader, I am very passionate about educating and teaching women the act of self-permission. As a woman that once poured all her love into others with nothing to show for herself, this act was very foreign to me because I believed in the idea that you must love others before you can love yourself. Yes, it is important to show compassion, kindness, and love toward others, but how are you supposed to do this truly if you don't even show true love to yourself? I got this part wrong for many years. Since the "leftover love" I gave myself was so crap, I wasn't actually giving soul love. In today's society, the idea is that if you love yourself first then you are selfish or an egotistical person. This idea and lie around self-love infuriates me to my core! Loving yourself first isn't selfish or egotistical. It is vital because if you don't love yourself first with real and true love, respect, value, and appreciation for yourself then really the love you are giving others isn't come from a place of authenticity, so really how pure is the love your giving?

When you tend to your self-love tank, you're able to love others bigger, better, and brighter! Please dear reader, don't fall into this trap. Make sure that you love yourself first, then go love others. Please don't settle for leftover love! You are worthy to have and feel so much self-love in your heart and soul. Start your Self-Love for the Soul journey today, beautiful, and go sparkle bright.

💜 Nicole Curtis

## Melissa Dickson

Entrepreneur/Founder of Melissa Dickson

https://www.facebook.com/profile.php?id=100086677090831
https://www.instagram.com/melissadickson888/
www.melissadickson.com.au

Melissa is an entrepreneur, mother, business owner, author and a passionate women's advocate. She shares some of her passions in her books 'Green Home Cleaning' and 'You're Not Crazy', Melissa has built a brand around her strong passion for inspiring women to believe in themselves and supports them to create time and financial freedom.

Today, when she's not listening to country music, reading books or creating memories with her children, you'll often find her having a positive impact in the lives of others, helping the planet and inspiring women to believe in themselves.

To learn more about Melissa and how she can help you create time and financial freedom visit www.melissadickson.com.au

# I'M WORTH A MILLION DOLLARS - KNOW YOUR WORTH!

By Melissa Dickson

What does it mean to know your worth?

I wasn't bought by anyone, so what does that mean?

Self-esteem, self-worth, self-reflection, know your worth—these are all words and phrases we hear often, but do we truly understand their meaning?

I asked all the same questions while becoming a mother, so here is a summary of my learnings.

As a busy mother, I was feeling very overwhelmed and stressed. The greatest gift I have ever received is being a mother. My children are my blessings, and I am so grateful to be their mum. However, somehow, since becoming a mother, my personal identity has almost completely faded. My life was so entangled in following social norms, living up to others' expectations, and the day-to-day activities of life that I forgot to reflect, and before I knew it, I was in a vicious circle.

Getting kids ready for school or childcare and the dreaded school run, then the mad dash to work, cleaning and preparing dinner, laundry—Wash-Dry-Fold-Repeat—after school activities, navigating emotions in children, catering to everyone's needs, and completing everyday chores.

My question quickly became, who am I?

As for the real me, who am I?

It's not me as a mother, wife, cleaner, chef, counselor, but me as the incredible woman I am.

In what way does she wish to be fulfilled?

What are her dreams?

Are there any goals she wants to achieve?

As I reflected on my life, I was also experiencing constant abdominal pain, fatigue, and nausea and was often bedridden. Despite my best efforts, I couldn't walk to the kitchen because of my sharp hip pain. My doctor was consulted about this ongoing health concern. To find the cause, I was referred to several specialists, and years passed.

As the surgical and medication process progressed, a guessing game followed.

As a result of my first major surgery, I was diagnosed with two diseases. After hearing this, I felt a lot of relief. Due to what I had learned and understood, I was able to make informed health decisions. I could also better understand the symptoms I had been experiencing and how to manage them. I also gained a better understanding of the risks associated with each diseaseand the importance of staying informed about my health. After becoming stressed and experiencing declining health due to my role as a working mother and student, I began the self-reflection process of changing my lifestyle. In my mind, I remember thinking: *how could I have let this happen to me? I am so far from the person I truly am.* It would be a learning curve here, so I knew I would have to take it step by step.

Working and studying for my degree meant I had to manage a full course load while also managing my health, so understanding my diagnosis was paramount. I had to work hard to balance my time and energy between studying, working, mothering, and my health.

After pondering in self-reflection for a few weeks, my answers began to emerge. I identified my weaknesses and developed a plan to strengthen them. I also recognized my strengths and decided to focus on putting them to use. I was determined to stay true to myself and use this experience to grow. I began journaling and changed the words I used both internally and externally. During my commute, I listened to Louise Hay's audiobooks over and over again. A part of me also wanted to positively impact the lives of others and our beautiful planet. Living low-tox, having abundance, enjoying life right now, and living consciously became my values, and I wanted to align my life with those values.

In order to make my home as low toxic as possible, I started making changes. While researching detoxing my environment, I was horrified to learn that shampoo, food, pots and pans, chest rub, and even water from our taps can contain toxic chemicals. I gradually swapped items and became more health conscious. In light of all the updated information I found, I decided to better my health. My holistic health-conscious choices allowed me to become disease-free, and I am thankful for that.

For the first time in my life, I started taking extra care of myself. I created a self-care list and embraced the belief that I could give more if my cup was full. It was a challenge at first for me to take care of myself because I believed I wasn't worthy of those things. This was far from the truth at the time.

Self-care is often associated with massages, flowers, manicures, and pedicures, and let me not mislead you; these are all valuable and necessary. I believe self-care goes beyond this and includes all aspects of one's life. In addition to setting boundaries, saying no to others, speaking your truth, having time for yourself, and saying yes to yourself, self-care is all about you!

Physical, mental, emotional, social, spiritual, and financial aspects are all part of holistic self-care. It is important to take the time to prioritize these aspects of your life and invest in yourself. You deserve to take the time to nourish and nurture your body, mind, and soul. Self-care is a necessary part of life that allows us to feel our best.

Taking care of oneself holistically is extremely important to reduce anxiety, depression, and stress.

In addition to increasing energy, it increases resilience and happiness as well.

You need to care for your physical well-being to maintain an efficient body. The body and mind are closely connected, so when a body is healthy, it will think and feel better. Physical self-care recommendations include exercise, yoga, eating healthy food and drink, sleeping enough each night, arranging your living space, setting goals for what you want to accomplish, taking time for yourself, pursuing hobbies, and knowing your morals and values.

In addition to breathing, eating, digesting, seeing, hearing, smelling, tasting, dancing, running, singing, talking, reproducing, and storing our souls, our bodies are our sacred temples.

My sacred temple, my body, thank you for being there for me.

You gave birth to my children after keeping them alive for nine months while they grew and developed.

I am thankful for my sight so that I can see flowers, my children's faces, cows, nature, and so much more.

As I listen to my country music, hear kookaburras sing each morning, and hear my loved ones' voices, I am grateful for my hearing.

Having the opportunity to sample different foods and drinks is a blessing to me.

You have given me the voice to express my truth and sing along to the songs I love.

I would like to thank you for spreading love throughout the world through my heart.

I am grateful for my sense of smell so that I can experience the scent of freshly mowed lawns and freshly baked muffins.

I am grateful for my intuition, for my 'just knowing.'

Having you as my temple for four decades has been an honor. I would like to thank you, thank you, thank you. My gratitude is endless.

It's important to acknowledge and express your feelings regularly and safely in order to maintain your emotional well-being. Expressing uncomfortable emotions such as anger and sadness in a healthy way is crucial for feeling good. Self-care activities for emotional well-being include reflecting on emotions, journaling, creating art, playing music, expressing yourself, challenging negative thinking, and identifying triggers.

As a part of my emotional self-love journey, I have learned to not worry about what others think of me. In the past, I cared deeply about others' opinions! It's no longer important to me what other people think because I am my own judge. Since I know myself better than anyone else, it does not pay to care too much about their opinions of me.

I am constantly getting to know myself a bit more each day. When I think about what matters to me most, I consider what I value most. Reflecting on my history reveals the path I have traveled and the evolution I have undergone as a human.

Since I am the only one who knows what inspires and drives me, I am unstoppable when it comes to my imagination and creativity. Writing down my goals helps me become more aware of what I want in life. My life doesn't have to follow the path other people suggest. Ultimately, I am responsible for my own feelings. Regardless of what others say, I choose to turn a negative into a positive or an opportunity to learn and grow. Only I can make me truly, deeply happy.

Being perfectly me….

Raw, real, imperfect me…

Taking care of one's social self requires maintaining a social network. A strong network of friends, family, and colleagues is essential for emotional health and professional growth. Nurturing relationships by staying in touch and engaging in meaningful conversations is important. Social connections provide a source of support, a sense of belonging, and a feeling of community. Maintaining close relationships and socializing is important to any self-care regimen. Engage in activities that nurture your relationship with others, stop comparing yourself with others, and spend time with your friends.

Social self-care learnings have taught me I have no time for gossiping, negativity, or putting others down.

For me, it's not negotiable!

The concept of spiritual self-care is about nurturing your spirit, and it doesn't have to be religious. Any activity that helps you develop a deeper sense of meaning, understanding, or connection to the universe can be included. The health of your spirit can be nurtured by activities such as meditation, prayer, being in nature, and practicing mindfulness. The practice of meditation has become a part of my life, and I love it!

In my world, deep conversations are the best...

Deep, engaging, exciting, and thirsty discussions.

Being motivated to do better is what I'm talking about.

In the conversations that I feel in my soul, I can see it in the expressions.

There's nothing more authentic, raw, and real than that!

Financial self-care is equally important as all other areas of self-care. It's necessary to take control of your finances, to be mindful of your spending, and to plan for the future. Financial self-care is about ensuring you are in charge, not the other way around. It's about making sure your money is working for you. The habits, beliefs, and rituals you follow contribute to achieving your financial goals. You can stimulate your financial situation by participating in financial planning, cultivating a deeper relationship with money, setting empowering money goals, showing gratitude, creating a budget, learning about money mindset, reading financial books, and having regular money dates with yourself. I discovered I had a generational subconscious belief that money was evil and difficult to come by. After becoming aware of this, I cultivated a deeper relationship with money by reprogramming my money mindset.

Finally, making regular time for yourself can help you create healthier habits and attitudes. It can also help you become more productive and creative in your life and work.

Taking time for yourself can be as simple as taking a few moments to meditate, walk, or read a book. It can also involve scheduling time for activities that bring you joy, such as cooking, painting, or playing a musical instrument. These activities can help you to clear your mind and refocus your energy.

Finding a balance between caring for the family and oneself is essential for a healthy and happy life.

Setting boundaries and establishing a routine is key to finding balance and avoiding burnout. Prioritizing yourself and your needs is important to set yourself up for success. Regularly checking in with yourself and reflecting on what is important to you can help you stay on track.

My journey so far has been such an adventure, and I have learned a lot.

Each and every one of us has ups and downs in life, and I am grateful for all of them.

My personal development journey has introduced me to many wonderful books and inspiring speakers and let me understand how powerful self-reflecting can be.

This journey has taught me that I have the power to make my life what I want it to be—that no one else can limit me. I'm so grateful to have this knowledge and excited to continue growing and learning more.

In my life, I have learned lessons, grown, and evolved into a better version of myself.

Throughout this process, I have learned a lot about myself.

It is imperative for me to accept myself for who I am, love myself, and take proper holistic care of myself.

As a result of my journey of learning, I am extremely passionate about inspiring others to live their dreams and believe in themselves. To make a positive difference in people's lives and to protect our beautiful planet, I founded a company and brand. Through these platforms, I inspire and encourage people to be bold, brave, and, most importantly, true to themselves. In my business, I've partnered with an organization that's been around for 50 years and aligns with my values: Being environmentally friendly, Living a low-tox lifestyle, ensuring my children inherit abundance and a legacy, making a positive difference in other people's lives, living life with time freedom, recognizing the importance of living consciously, and making a positive contribution to a better world.

I absolutely love what I do because I get to have positive impacts on other people's lives, have positive impacts on the environment, and create time, freedom, and abundance in the world.

The value of abundance in my life allows me to positively impact the lives of others.

My value of time freedom is that I can do what I want when I want and being able to set my own schedule.

Living consciously means being aware of how my decisions impact my body, mind, spirit, and the planet. There is nothing like this experience!

As an author, business owner, and advocate for self-love. I strive to inspire others to achieve their dreams and live freely. All of this was built on my belief in myself, my self-love, and my belief that I am worth it.

Don't underestimate your value!

Regardless of what life throws your way, always remember your dreams and desires are just as valid as anyone's.

YOU ARE WORTHY!

## Magalie Delisle

Think Wise Live Free
Godly Wifehood & Financial Wisdom Coach

https://www.facebook.com/groups/thinkwiselivefree
https://www.instagram.com/magaliedelisle7
https://youtube.com/@ThinkWiseLiveFree

Magalie Delisle is a passionate caregiver and biblical online business builder. In 1996 and 2003, she went through heavy mental illness issues. But her faith saved her. She started her caregiving career in 2020 when the pandemic started. She almost lost her job even though she's an essential worker because she cares "too much" about health freedom. So she decided to start an online business to wisely get a second source of income.

Today, when she's not running after elders to shower them, you'll often find her helping wives follow God's instructions for their marriage and build biblical home business as Proverb 31 woman.

To learn more about Magalie on how she overcame mental illness roadblocks and how she can help you get back your time/financial freedom, to become your husband's help meet you where created to be, join her Facebook group and subscribe to her YouTube channel.

# RISE AS QUEEN ESTHER

By Magalie Delisle

## Isolated From The Isolated

The belt tightened my wrists, ankles, and waist. I was naked. I tried to move to save myself, but I was literally pinned to the bed. The next day, my husband, whom I had left for another man, visited me as he did every day. He cared for his wife with free, faithful love, without asking to be loved in return. That day, for a change, I wanted him as my husband. I saw him coming from the other side of the door, but it wasn't visiting time, so the guard stopped him from entering. I panicked. Other guards locked me in a room two meters by two meters with a simple blue mattress on the floor. I screamed until I had no voice. I was in isolation, isolated from the isolated, in a psychiatric hospital room. I was 27 years old in 2003. It was my second psychotic episode; the first had occurred in 1996 when I was 20 years old.

## Secured By Death

I was born into a non-practicing Catholic family. My childhood was very difficult. My mother was being beaten by her boyfriend. I was terrified to find her dead after school. I was running away to an imaginary world to protect myself from pain. One morning, I almost fainted on an ordinary school day. I don't know why I looked at the time and remembered it, but I did. That evening when I got home, I learned that my favorite uncle had committed suicide at the exact same time. I understood that there's a spiritual world and that one can be sensitive to it. I began to be fascinated by death. Strangely enough, I was somehow secured by the idea of death. Because I could finally rely on something that was 100% certain to happen, it gave me stability in my thoughts. I've read a lot about near-death experiences. That's how I started my spiritual quest.

**Baring My Soul**

I looked for God everywhere, in a Hindu sect, a secret society and mediums. Then mental illness came in without knocking at the door. I was delirious. The characters on TV were talking to me looking directly at me. (Zoom didn't exist yet!) I had the sensation of being a centaur, of giving birth to a snake, of having the voice of a man and of having a radio in my head that was impossible to turn off. My body was burning like I was on fire. I heard infernal screams from the hairdryer. One day I decided to go on strike from eating, sleeping and washing. I peed in my bed. I often had sleep paralysis and felt like I was being raped, but there was no one there. When I was awake I had dream consciousness, when I was asleep I had waking consciousness. I thought I was the only one going through this, but today, I know I'm not. I'm baring my soul, so if you've experienced something similar, now you know you're not alone.

**The Psychiatric Floor**

My mother took me to the hospital emergency room. The doctor wanted to keep me, but I wanted to go home. He convinced me to just visit the psychiatric floor, but when I saw the numbers on the wall and that I needed a code to get out of there (which I didn't have), I panicked. That's one of the ways I earned the bed restraint. My soul was suffering so much that I asked my psychiatrist to euthanize me. The law didn't allow him to kill me at that time, so he refused. But can you imagine that in Canada, our government is discussing passing a law that would allow doctors to euthanize people suffering from mental illnesses? I would've died at 20… without knowing Jesus my savior or my husband. Yet as a passionate caregiver, I help so many sick people! Hey, I know you must feel like garbage if you're in the midst of mental illness right now, but you're NOT!!!

## Medication

I was released from the hospital with a lifetime prescription of strong medication. I came back with my husband and built a stable life. I consulted a Jungian psychoanalyst for five years. I wanted to solve my problem at the source. Medication only froze my suffering. It was during this time that I met my savior Jesus, and He delivered me from many tormenting demons. If you want details about my healing, I encourage you to watch my complete testimony on YouTube (Link at the end). Today, I don't take any medication for mental illness anymore. But I don't advise anyone to go off their medication lightly. Before changing anything on my prescription, I wanted to have my doctor's approval and follow up on everything. So I waited until I had thoughts, emotions, and life stability. Then my doctor lowered my prescription little by little over several years. It took about five years before I stopped completely. Today, I have a clear mind, without side effects. I'm building my online business as an affiliate marketer and soon, as a biblical mindset coach. I've started my online journey by believing I'd make 20k in my second month. I was wrong. So please, be wiser than me and know that you'll have to put in efforts to build a business. Even the simplest business model requires effort. What's the simplest way to start? Affiliate marketing because you don't have to craft your own offer. You get an affiliate link from an existing product you're passionate about and when someone buys from it, you get commission. You can be an affiliate for just about any company like Amazon or Walmart. If you want to learn more about this simple business model, follow the steps at the end of my chapter.

## Neighbors And Self-Love

"But what in the world has someone not able to control a single thought and feeling in the past, doing creating a biblical mindset coaching program?" you may ask. Well, where the human flesh has been cut deeply, a scar appears. The skin of this scar becomes stronger and harder than the normal skin that has not been injured! That happened to my mind, which became one of my strengths. I like the title of this book, because the Bible teaches we shall love our neighbor as ourselves. I've found that because I didn't love myself, I was not able to love my neighbors. I was so overwhelmed by my own suffering that I truly loved no one. But after I was delivered, I began to be very active in helping others rather than just thinking about myself. I taught children in church and visited psychiatric patients to show them living proof that you can get through this. Then I found my first vocation and went back to school at 43 to become a caregiver. When I'm with these lovely elders, I don't feel like I'm trading time for money. But during the pandemic, I've almost lost my job and marriage. This crisis has caused me to rethink my mindset about my wifehood and money-making activity.

**Work At Home**

I realize that often, Christians, myself included, say that they believe in the Bible from beginning to end while rejecting certain parts. Sometimes we pick and choose what suits us and reject some other parts, thinking that it's no longer for us or of our time. We contradict ourselves, don't we? So during this identity crisis I decided to believe a bible verse that I'd previously rejected. The one that says wives should work at home and be keepers at home. Don't get me wrong, I love caregiving and I'll always care for elders in one way or another. But I've found that a wife being forced to work for a foreign boss 40h/week is unhealthy for couples. It creates extra work for both, and frustration. It's a real slavery of our time for money. Sadly, women have to earn money by wasting valuable time outside the home. And men have to do household chores, losing precious time for their mission. As a result, the couple doesn't build anything worthwhile as a team, each one ambitiously goes his own way. Couples and children suffer. You're probably an ambitious woman, so why not start that home business you've been dreaming of? Eventually, you'll be able to work the hours that suit you, make the money you need, and more. With this time freedom, you'll be able to put your priorities in the right place. Let's be honest, your heart's first priority is God and your family, but in your daily activity, your priority is your 9-5 job isn't it?

**Behind Great Men**

Each man has a mission, but a husband without a wife available to help him as a team partner will not go far. Do you think that the women in the phrase "Behind every great man, there's a woman" were women who worked from 9-5 for a stranger? NO! They were present, available for their man. Were these women entrepreneurs? YES! For example, the woman in Proverb 31 from the Bible was a woman who first took care of her family, then with the free time she had left, she was doing business. Her way of making money didn't force her to put family second in her daily activities. She did not trade her precious time for money. She gave her best productive time to her husband and children first. Behind every great man is a woman with time freedom to devote to her man's great mission.

**Escape Plan**

"Oh, I want time freedom for my husband and kids! But we absolutely need my second income to manage to pay for everything. I can't quit my job overnight!" you might say. You're totally right! You need an escape plan first, that you can build together with your husband. Start by cleaning up your mindset and daily activities outside of your 9-5 schedule. Meaning, ditch false beliefs, make room in your thoughts to review your priorities, make room in your personal activities to embark on a progressive life-changing journey. The best way to change your mindset is by studying the life of Queen Esther. And the best way to begin this life changing journey is to model the Proverbs 31 woman's priorities, one step at a time.

**Rise As Queen Esther**

What might this escape plan from your 9-5 job look like? Start by being grateful for everything this job gives you, financially and personally. What skills have you learned? What soul transformation have you gone through? Let's look briefly at the life of Queen Esther. Esther was a young Jewish orphan and slave who was taken as a candidate for royalty. The king chose her as queen without knowing she was Jewish. While a plot to exterminate the Jews took place, she courageously rose to save them. This ordinary girl became a queen for such a time as this, to help the Jews escape from death. What if there was a specific group of people just waiting for you to rise? You were created with talents, abilities, and skills that no one else has. And there's a group of people associated with your specific mission. They literally need you to improve their lives. They have a problem, and you have the solution. This group is already willing to pay you for access to the solution you can offer. So my friend, rise as Esther for your audience's sake and start this business you dream of.

**Proverb 31 Woman's Priorities**

I know your schedule must already be overloaded with your 40h work week and family demands. Getting Proverb 31 woman lifestyle is a transformative process and we don't all start at the same level. It's okay! It requires commitment. Some people even go so far as to invest money to hire a coach. Let's look closer at this virtuous woman's life who sometimes seems too perfect to be modeled. What are her priorities? God of course, but then? Does she get up every morning to submit herself to a foreign boss's will in exchange for salary? One of the first things mentioned about her is: her husband trusts her, she's a great asset to him, and meets his needs. Did you notice that it's not her boss who benefits from her value but her husband? Who did you fall in love with and marry? Shouldn't your husband receive the submission of your time and skills rather than your boss?

**Proverb 31 Woman's Activities**

Now let's see what this valuable woman's daily activities are. The proverb says that she does good to her husband every day, she works with her hands, she brings food for family from afar (probably to find quality and bargains), she buys a field, she plants a vineyard with her earnings. She sells clothes and belts. She's a businesswoman who can afford to have servants. She reaches out to the poor, she oversees the running of her house, she's an action taker. She has other priorities than trading her precious time for salary; she's a free woman. Is this unattainable? It's impossible to achieve overnight. Creating a priority management plan can bring about an impressive life change! To do so, start by freeing up a special time every day, at least every week, fixing your mindset. A mentor or coach can also help you accelerate the pace toward this accomplishment. Be both determined and gracious to yourself.

**An Invitation**

My friend, it's time for you to rise as Queen Esther! Get back your time freedom to help your husband in his God-given mission in priority. Commit to rescue your specific God-given group to serve. So if your heart's priority is family, but your 9-5 job comes first in your daily activity, you're not alone! If you and your hubby are overwhelmed by your chaotic schedule, not building anything worthwhile as a team, each one of you going ambitiously his own way, don't worry! If you absolutely need your second income to manage your finances, if you feel your talents and abilities are wasted, not having time to answer this calling to start your business, this invitation is for you. Join my Facebook group and subscribe to my YouTube channel. There you'll find encouragement, tips, and recommendations helping you to rise courageously and make that life changing decision of starting a biblical home business. You'll find guidance through the process of modeling

Proverb 31 woman's lifestyle one step at a time. Ready to walk in complete Freedom? Then take these 3 simple meaningful actions:

1. Launch An Affiliate Marketing Home Business In Just 72 Hours
2. Join My Facebook Group To Grab "The 9-5 Escape Plan For Proverb 31 Women" The Marriage Savior
3. Subscribe To My YouTube Channel To Learn More About "The 9-5 Escape Plan For Proverb 31 Women"

Access Everything Here:
https://linktr.ee/thinkwiselivefree

## Katie Tschida

KRT Virtual Assistant. LLC
Digital Organizer

https://www.linkedin.com/in/krtvirtualassistant/
www.facebook.com/krtvirtualassistant
www.instagram.com/krtvirtualassistant
www.krtvirtualassistant.com
links.krtvirtualassistant.com

Katie Tschida is a homeschooling mom to 3 kids who, in 2020, decided to take the plunge and become an entrepreneur.

She has since specialized as a digital organizer and accountability assistant, helping business owners tame their overflowing inboxes and meet their goals. With her assistance, business owners can keep a sense of organization and direction in their work.

Katie loves to travel and create memories with her family. She believes that the experiences gained through travel can be a valuable learning opportunity for all.

Katie's mission is to help business owners streamline their processes to maximize their time and energy. With her help, her clients can free up their time to focus on what matters most, achieve their goals, and spend quality time with their families.

# THE HARDEST BATTLE OFF THE FIELD

By Katie Tschida

War is easy to start, hard to end, and impossible to forget. My time in the US Army will stay with me forever. The toughest war I've had to face today, though, is the one with myself.

Being in the Army taught me many things, like how to fold socks into balls harder than rocks and how to stand up for your rights against your superiors. It taught me the importance of organization and being on top of your tasks so you can be one step ahead. It never prepared me to deal with the chaos after. For me, it's the chaos of juggling motherhood and entrepreneurship.

On paper, doing the two seems simple. As a mom, you feed your children, love them, and guide them to be decent human beings. As an entrepreneur, you follow your passion and execute it in a way to help others. Your organization gets thrown out the window when these two personas overlap, though. Knowing what to do in theory is one thing, and having an actionable plan is another. As one baby turned into two, I figured out how to balance motherhood and entrepreneurship. It got easier as they got older and more independent.

That was the lie I told myself.

Over the years, the tasks got easier because I created more time by sacrificing something—a good night's sleep. I trained my body to sleep for five hours a day, then convinced my mind that that was enough. It was enough to get me through the day and do what I needed to get done. Take the kids to gymnastics. Do some client work. Cook dinner. Spend some time with my husband. Break up the fight in the kitchen because someone spilled water!

On one day in particular, I slept in by a few hours. As I rolled over and looked at the clock, I noticed the time.

"Shoot!" I yelled as I scurried out of bed. *"Shoot! Shoot! Shoot! I'm behind on my day!"* I thought as I hurried out of my bedroom, but then it hit me.

My bronchial pneumonia started to act up. "I'll fight my way through it," I told myself. "I've been through worse," encouraging my mind and body that it would be okay. It had to be okay because there was so much to do!

As I fought through my day, my cough got worse. I still convinced myself to get one more task done. And one more for good measure. I was already behind, so I pushed on.

*You need to rest,* a voice in my head said. Sighing, I accepted that my subconscious was right. It'll only get worse if I don't. So I consulted with my planner to see what could be moved around. My heart dropped while looking at everything that needed to get done. My body started to pulse with anxiety as my blood started to sprint. Then, my cough started acting up again. I covered my mouth with clammy palms and knew what was happening.

I experienced this in basic training before. During my Army days in basic training, I was so scared of falling behind that I pushed myself hard. I convinced myself that I was a warrior who didn't need to take care of myself. *I'm fine.* But I wasn't. The doctor told me that if I had pushed myself a little more, precisely five more days, I wouldn't be here anymore.

The thought of no longer being here made my blood run cold. If I had overtaxed myself back then, my kids wouldn't be here. So what would happen if I kept pushing myself now? I thought about it for some time and listened to what my body told me. *Slow down.* If I kept pushing, my body would fail again. I'd get gravely sick and be useless, so it was time to take care of myself.

My mind raged ware against my body. It kept fighting against my body, reminding me what I needed to cross off my list. *So what could I do?*

Being the organizer that I am, I bit back my anxiety and looked at my planner. My body screamed at me that it was time to make adjustments with every painful cough. I needed to stop running myself ragged. I did this to myself in basic training, and my superiors forced me to rest. Back then, I had caring superiors to look over me. Now, the only person I had to hold my health accountable was me.

Recently, I started taking on more in hopes of advancing my business. As a business owner, I need to plan out all the tasks to keep my business running. Some of my tasks included showing up daily and creating new content. This didn't include promoting and connecting with new clients. Marketing, alone, takes time to plan, design, and execute. Yet here I was, pushing it out as fast as I could because I was encouraged to do so. That strategy works for some people, but it doesn't work for everybody. It didn't for me.

My health tanked. My energy drained to almost zero, and it was time to listen to my body and slow down. I needed to slow down for myself, my family, and the people I love. That's when it dawned on me that I didn't need a get-rich plan to be happy. My happiness and good health made me wealthy, so I made the conscious decision to start taking care of myself.

Building a business and working towards financial freedom is a wonderful goal, but in the long run, family comes first. My family always comes first, which is why I started focusing on myself. I asked myself what I needed and what to do at that moment. Surprisingly, the answer came quickly. Break the habit of putting everyone and everything first and myself last. Instead, flip the script and put me first. Everything else will fall into place after. This was my first act of self-love. It wasn't easy, but I learned to respect myself.

Loving yourself is not selfish. Loving yourself involves reminding yourself that you are valuable. You are deserving despite your flaws and mistakes. You can do it. You are worthy of self-love, and your overall well-being will ignite when you do love yourself. Your self-esteem will skyrocket. Loving myself allowed me to start living a fulfilling life. My fulfilling life allowed me to provide for everyone better than you could ever imagine.

If you can't benefit from loving yourself, how can you expect anyone else to?

**Carol Bustamante**

Intutition 0f Light
Psychic Intuitive, Energy Healer

https://www.facebook.com/carol.beckerbustamante/
www.instagram.com/Intuition_0f_Light
www.carolbustamante.com

Hello People of the Universe and welcome to my energy! I am Carol Bustamante Psychic Intuitive and Vibrational Healer. I am all about love, light, forgiveness and healing. And I am all about guiding people into their heart light so that they can live more of a balanced loving life. We all are light vibrational beings!

I have been doing Readings and energy attunements for over 25 years. I absolutely love what I do and love people. My journey getting here wasn't easy, I've made many mistakes along the way. And little did I know back then that I was creating from a wounded place. After many tears and frustrations, I finally surrendered all of what was laying heavy in my heart. I decided to take a different approach, changed my mindset, and let go of what no longer served me. Now, I am living a heart centered life!

# I AM LOVE MADE MANIFEST

By Carol Bustamante

Hello people of the universe, I'm Carol Bustamante, a psychic intuitive and energy therapist. I am all about love, light, and frequency. Welcome to my energy! I am excited about this self-love project. It is aligned with what I do and who I have become. My life was not all roses and champagne. I have had many setbacks and heartaches in my life, and I wasn't always positive, or should I say I didn't have a positive mindset. I didn't have as much love, clarity, and strength for myself as I do now. This journey to self-love was not an easy one for me. I had a very strong will and ego, and I was trying to control everything in my life. How did that work out for me? It didn't. I found myself exhausted and drained like a battery about to lose its power. I was always searching for the next charge or boost to uplift myself. Food was my drug. I use food to make myself feel better, and for a time, it helped. Until it did not. Looking back, I used food to shove down my feelings and to numb myself out. I was not living in my own truth—my own self-love. In fact, I created a deception for myself that I had no idea I was doing until I took the road of healing. I was self-sabotaging myself with a lack of self-love by overeating. I wasn't connected to the true essence of my being, my true nature, or my soul. I felt so overwhelmed with pain and emotion. I knew I needed to take a different approach than before. I truly had to take a deep look in the mirror at myself and the lies I was accepting as my truth. Right around the time I was thinking this to myself, my cousin pulled me aside and asked me, "Have you looked in the mirror? Do you realize that you need to take action with your health?" Do you want to watch your two young, beautiful boys grow up?" And that's when it all came crashing over me. I was 250 lbs with a 53-inch waist ( size 4X) at 5'5". I had hypertension, diabetes, and I needed a sleep apnea machine to help me breathe at night, AND I was only 35. I questioned myself. How did I get here? I felt a painful surge within me, like a strange release of anger, frustration, disgust, acknowledgement, love, and surrender. I fell to my knees, crying over the life I have created for myself and thought: no one is coming to save me. And I told myself, this is it; I must find a way out of the prison I put myself in. I released so much pent-up old emotion and stagnant energy that day. My head and eyes hurt from crying. And for the first time in a long time, I felt my body aching and telling me all this time to stop my lack of love for myself. And then I finally surrendered and was able to gather myself together, wipe away my tears, and take a big deep breath. I started to pray again and connect back to God. I asked, where do I go from here? How am I going to change? Who can help me? I prayed for healing and guidance. I prayed for strength and courage.

A month or so has passed since my energetic purge. I started researching weight loss surgery because I had tried so many diets and fads and nothing seemed to help. I went on obesityhelp.com and dove into all the information about the lap band and the Roux NY Gastric bypass. I read many stories about people's successes and failures. I thought, if I am going to do this, I am learning everything about it, so I can make a well-educated decision and feel good about it. I kept on seeing one doctor over and over with great reviews. Doctor Capella was known for the Roux NY Gastric bypass and patient success rate. He was the only surgeon that took it to the next level and applied a band around the stoma( where the stomach and esophagus) . Why? Because patients would feel fuller, and you can overstuff or stretch out the tissue. I was also afraid to make the appointment, but I was determined to gather my strength.

A week passed by, and I was invited to a $4^{th}$ of July party at my cousin's house. It was a usual fun party, but ths time my cousin introduced me to his new girlfriend. I didn't know it at that time, but she was my angel back then. An answer to one of my prayers. I met Paula and we hit it off. She was sweet and petite, and I felt comfortable with her. We got to talking, and I told her I loved her outfit and mentioned I would love to wear that, but I am a size 4X. And I couldn't believe what came out of her mouth. "I was once like you, but bigger." ( she was a 5X at 450lbs.) My ears opened up even more. So I asked her, how did you lose all that weight? She said she had the Roux NY Gastric bypass, and her surgeon was excellent. She told me her doctor was Dr. Capella, and he does it slightly differently from other surgeons. My jaw dropped, and I couldn't believe what I was hearing! I told her I was thinking about doing it because I had so many comorbidities, and I wanted to live a healthier life. She was excited for me and told me to schedule a consultation with him. And so I did! Prayer one, answered.

The consultation day came, and I was nervous, but it felt right. His staff was efficient and kind. He went over everything, and I agreed. He offered his patients a support group that met weekly with new and existing patients. They talked about their struggles and how they dealt with their weight loss. This felt so good. It felt right, and I knew then my life was going to change. I knew it was not going to be easy. I had a long road ahead, but I was determined to change, grow, and start loving myself more. This changed my life in a huge, unpredictable way. I knew I had to change my thoughts, my behaviors, my mindset, and my actions if I wanted to be a newer, fresher version of me. My family supported me in my decision.

Fast forward, I had the surgery, and all went very well. I had no infections and followed the doctor's instructions to the letter! I drank 4-5 protein shakes a day for a month, and within three months I dropped 60lbs, and I was so cranky. HA! This journey was tough and gritty, but I wasn't giving up. I stayed in my lane and lost more. I felt really weird with the weight being gone, and when I passed a mirror, I didn't know who was looking back (body dysmorphia). I started forgiving and loving myself a little more every day. I took up walking three miles a day, drinking a lot of water, and I made a vow to myself that I would continue being the better version of myself. I changed my relationship with food and kept my promise to continue attending support group meetings. I grew more responsible and accountable for my actions while purging emotions. My body was changing on the outside, and I was also changing on the inside, and it was all happening so fast. For the first time in a long time, I felt really good physically and mentally.

I have learned so much about myself during this time. I realized I was putting everyone else before me and my needs. I learned to be accountable and responsible for everything in my life. And most of all, I learned to love myself on a deeper level. My mindset is clearer and more positive than ever, and my relationship with food has changed for the better. I respect myself, and I am proud of the choices I have made. It's been over 20 years since my surgery and new way of being, and I am happy to tell you that I maintain a healthy 120 lbs, size 4. My hypertension went away, along with my diabetes, and all my body aches. I exercise, walk, and maintain a healthy lifestyle. But most importantly, this journey was more of a soulful journey of enlightenment—a journey into my heart center and the love that I am. It was and still is about my relationship with myself and my soul. I believe in miracles and prayer, and most of all, I believe in the power of love. Self-love saves the day!

I am love made manifest, and I have come to awaken this in you all.

—Lady Sarah

**Yvonne Wallin**

It Is All For You Solutions, LLC
Thriving Beyond Depression Coach/Owner

https://www.facebook.com/yvwall
www.instagram.com/thrivingbeyonddepressoin
www.thrivingbeyonddepression.com

Yvonne Wallin is a much sought after expert, coaching female leaders and entrepreneurs to leave frustration and depression behind, create a thriving life and future. After struggling with major depression, she pursued a master's degree in counseling, graduating in 2013. She specialized in equine assisted counseling and studying how to help those with depression and adult survivors of abuse. After graduating she decided to pursue certification in coaching and obtained a certification in 2014. She is currently in the process of completing another certification in woman centered coaching.

Today, when she is not enjoying time with friends and family or spending time outdoors working on the farm with the animals where she lives in the country, you will find her helping her coaching clients.

To learn more about Yvonne Wallin and how she can help you to leave frustration and depression behind, create a thriving life and future, visit www.thrivingbeyonddepression.com.

# LOVING YOURSELF AFTER DEPRESSION

By Yvonne Wallin

Self-love and depression. Can they co-exist? If you have experienced depression, you may ask if this is even possible.

Learning self-love is a continuous journey every day as we live life. We can learn to recognize when we move into self-love, away from the habitual place of depression, away from the negative thoughts cycling through our heads.

Am I here to tell you it will be easy? ABSOLUTELY NOT! However, it is possible, if you really want to end the frustration of feeling like you are going back into depression again and if you choose to create the necessary changes in your life.

So many people spend years with depression as a constant shadow in their lives, wondering if it will ever just go away. I know I did. Experiencing debilitating feelings of fear, dread, and worry, with negative thoughts cycling, feeling nothing about me was right. It took me years of therapy to get out of the depths, then continuous self-work until I could start enjoying things without just going through the motions of daily life. I was afraid of getting hooked on meds and their side effects. I decided not to take any anti-depressants, even though they were recommended because they can have varying degrees of effectiveness from person to person.

Your Self-Love journey begins when you start taking control, implementing new habits, and changing how you think. I had a poster as a teenager and into my twenties before it was damaged. It had the following quote from Mahatma Gandhi.

> Your beliefs become your thoughts.
> Your thoughts become your words.
> Your words become your actions.

Your actions become your habits.
Your habits become your values.
Your values become your destiny.

Becoming a coach was a culmination of various events I experienced. As a kid, my biggest dream was to have a horse, which finally occurred much later in my life. Jump forward about 15 or so years, and I was triggered by the events of 9/11, headlong into depression.

When I was a child, a couple of my family members attempted to commit suicide. One succeeded, and nobody ever really talked about it. This affected me so much that when I became depressed as an adult, it was difficult for me to acknowledge or even think about going to therapy. It was almost taboo in my head. Because I had never processed the memories of unresolved trauma from my childhood, 9/11 triggered these memories. The feelings that surged, spiraling me into depression, were fear, abandonment, aloneness, and not knowing who to trust, which led to cycling thoughts.

After going through therapy and doing some self-work, which entailed a lot of reading about healing from depression and religious and self-help books by people like Tony Robbins, Wayne Dyer, and others, I soon learned about equine-assisted therapy. While taking horse riding lessons, I gained a lot of confidence working with these large, very reactive animals. I learned to be more present and became aware of their body language to understand them better and connect with them. I decided to pursue a degree in counseling specializing in equine-assisted therapy, studying how best to help adults with depression and survivors of childhood abuse. Then I decided to pursue coaching and helping women to thrive beyond depression and design their fulfilling life and future.

After going to therapy for depression, gratitude, mindfulness, and being grounded increased my Self-Love the most. These helped me start accepting myself and then start loving myself.

I've included some examples of these exercises:

GRATITUDE may seem simple, but it can be challenging. Even at our lowest, we can usually find something to be grateful for. Journal at least five, or more things to be grateful for morning and night. In the morning, it starts your day out positively, and at night it helps reframe your day in your mind to allow more peaceful sleep with less focus on things that normally cause the mind to cycle and worry.

MINDFULNESS and GROUNDING can be combined. These both can be useful when the mind is going in so many directions, and there is a need to become more present in the here and now.

I find Grounding useful to center myself before going into a mindfulness exercise. Picture your energy as strands extending outwards from you to every place and everyone you interacted with recently, and then picture those energy strands pulled back into your center. You may notice some of that energy is negative, and some is positive. Feel those two types of energy separate and focus on sending the negative energy shooting down out of the soles of your feet into the ground. At the same time, the earth is replenishing you with more positive grounding energy.

For the Mindfulness process, find something to focus on. It could be your breath, the cat in your lap, a plant, or something in nature if you are outside. As you focus, notice in detail what you are focusing on, becoming more in tune and connected. Spend time becoming more focused and then journal what you experience. Journal each time you do these exercises. Play with what you focus on and the amount of time you spend, and find what works for you.

Depression and Fear are some of the lowest emotions, while Self-Love, Peace, and Joy are some of the highest. How we feel depends on how we react to life's events and the meaning we give them. It is possible to influence our feelings more than we realize.

You can experience Self-Love if you really want to.

If you are experiencing clinical or major depression, please seek therapy. Find a local therapist or counselor or call one of the numbers below. I went to three or four before I found the person I felt comfortable talking with about my innermost private thoughts.

Depression Hotline 800-273-8255 (TALK)
Suicide Hotline 800-662-4357 (HELP)

## Melanie Grace Starr

Empower Your Potential with Melanie Starr
Woman's Empowerment & Trauma Transformation Coach

https://www.linkedin.com/in/melanie-starr-87850813/
https://www.facebook.com/healbraveandstrong
https://www.instagram.com/empower_your_potential_
www.empoweryourpotential.ca

Melanie Starr is a women's empowerment coach on a mission to help women heal and learn to love themselves deeply and unconditionally. She knows from her own personal experience how difficult it can be to heal our relationship with ourselves, as women, especially in the face of cultural conditioning, abuse, trauma, hardship and loss.

For nearly 30 years Melanie has pursued healing and spiritual growth through such pathways as yoga, Reiki, Emotional Freedom Techniques (tapping), qigong, breathwork, practical neuroscience and many other mind-body-heart-soul approaches. She weaves all of this wisdom into comprehensive holistic coaching programs to help women rise above their pasts and their conditioning to truly see and embrace themselves and their greater possibilities.

As a teacher, mentor, coach and healer, Melanie provides women with new skills, perspectives and healing experiences that empower them to fulfill their potential and thrive in deeply soul-satisfying lives.

# HOW ON EARTH
# AM I SUPPOSED TO LOVE MYSELF?

By Melanie Grace Starr

In my coaching and therapeutic work with women, I am saddened to see how often women find it impossible to speak three simple words: "I love myself."

I use a powerful healing process called Emotional Freedom Techniques (EFT tapping) that requires clients to say, "Even though _____ (whatever is causing them pain), I deeply and completely love and accept myself." Many women balk at this. Resistance comes up like a brick wall, and they just can't say it. To take the edge off, I redirect them to say, "I'm open to the *possibility* that I could *learn* to love myself." This is more realistic. They can get the words out. This opens a window in their hearts that allows self-love to enter, IF they believe learning to love themselves is important AND they commit to the process.

It's not just women in coaching or therapy who struggle to love themselves. A 2021 survey commissioned by The Body Shop and conducted by Ipsos found **half of women worldwide** feel more self-doubt than self-love, and 60 percent wish they had more respect for themselves.

Why do we, as women, have such a difficult time loving ourselves?

The answers could fill a book. I will highlight just a few:

It can be hard to love yourself when you're female because of attitudes you picked up about your worthiness in the cultural atmosphere. Some call it patriarchy; I call it societally entrenched misogyny. This comes partly from religious teachings that women are inferior, temptresses, and the undoing of men. In my generation and older, "good girls" sat with their knees together. It wasn't proper to like sex, and if you did, you were "bad"—never mind Mother Nature designed you to love sex! And, of course, women were not even legally recognized as persons in Canada until 1929. We were "chattels," property of men. There's more: being valued for appearance over character; impossible fake beauty standards; socialization to "be nice" and put our needs last; and economic undervaluation of women's traditional homemaking and child-raising roles.

On top of social conditioning, we have our personal experiences: internalizing parents' scolding to mean we are not good or worthy; childhood sexual abuse that made us feel ashamed; and abusive relationships that stripped us of our sense of worth. You get the idea.

It's an upstream swim to go from feeling fundamentally bad, unworthy, and less-than to truly accepting, loving, and celebrating who we are. But it's a swim we need to make to become the powerful creators Nature made us to be and to generate the lives of love and abundance we deserve.

In the face of programming that produces ingrained resistance to loving ourselves, it's important to take baby steps, or the resistance will stop you altogether.

It starts with having basic compassion for yourself as a human being who is suffering. You would have compassion for any other suffering being, so why not for yourself? Why judge or berate yourself for your lack of perfection or demand more from yourself than you would ask of anyone else?

Once you connect with compassion for yourself, you have an opening to forgive yourself for your mistakes and shortcomings. When you understand that 90 percent of your behaviour—including self-sabotage—is based on childhood programming below the level of conscious awareness, it's easier to forgive yourself.

Look inside to find your inner child, the innocent recipient of the programming. See her pain from living under a burden of self-denial, self-limitation, self-sabotage, and even self-destruction. Ask her what she needs from you now, and give it to her: understanding, kindness, and affection. Speak to your inner child as if you are her ideal all-loving mother. It really is a process of re-parenting yourself—not that your parents didn't love you, but they may not have known how to show their love in a way you could feel and accept.

I once asked a child psychologist what the most important thing for a parent to do is, and he said, "Notice the good!"

How would this play out in your re-parenting of yourself?

What do you notice? Do you focus on the good and reward yourself with kind words and experiences, or do you find fault and tear yourself down?

Pay close attention to how you speak to (and about) your adult self. When something unkind comes up, stop yourself. But please do not berate yourself for your unkind self-talk! That is also unkind. Instead, **apologize to yourself**, remind yourself you did not deserve that, and promise to be kinder to yourself. It helps to recognize how you think and speak is habitual, and it takes time and effort to change a habit.

Once you make a habit of thinking and speaking about yourself kindly, you will find it easier to open your heart to yourself. From here, you can start taking bigger steps, such as thanking yourself when you do something nice for yourself. This starts to produce a virtuous cycle of positive emotions, like appreciating yourself for how hard you work or how good you are at certain things. Like caring enough about yourself to set boundaries that protect your time and energy from people who don't appreciate you and don't return the same kind of energy to you that you give to them. Like caring enough about yourself to stop lying to yourself about the harmful choices you've been making and to make better decisions for yourself, whether in health, finances, or relationships. And then respecting yourself for your new decisions.

Do you see how you will start to feel proud of yourself? How shame will release from your being? How your heart will open to loving you?

It is not narcissism, self-indulgence, selfishness, or a sense of superiority that leads you to love yourself. It is the recognition that you, like everyone else, are an individual expression of all that is, a divine being, part of the fabric of the universe, and deserving of the same care and love as every other part of the fabric of the universe. It is the understanding that you cannot fully express and share the fullness of your divine gifts if you are cutting yourself off at the knees. If you are not there for yourself, you are underpowered, and you don't have much energy to give.

Another key to loving yourself is understanding that love is not just a feeling; it's an energy that permeates the universe. It's a frequency you can tune into and embody at a deep level. When you choose to see the world through the lens of love and let love rather than fear guide how you think, speak, and act, you will find that deep love for yourself naturally emerges.

In review: self-compassion, self-forgiveness, self-acceptance, self-respect, self-truthfulness, self-discipline… these are the seeds we plant to grow our self-love garden. Self-appreciation, self-care, self-trust, self-celebration, and self-love will soon bloom in glorious profusion. Blessed be!

**Stacey Short**

Founder of A Few Short Minutes Coaching

https://www.linkedin.com/in/afewshortminutes/
https://www.facebook.com/coachstaceyshort
https://www.instagram.com/afewshortminutes_coaching_/
www.afewshortminutescoaching.com

Stacey Short grew up an Air Force BRAT. She has always wanted to help others live a better life. In 2002, she graduated from the University of Oklahoma with a B.A. in Psychology. After discovering her newborn son was medically fragile in 2005, she pivoted back into the service industry to be able to better care for his medical needs. In 2016, she lost her baby brother to suicide. She struggled to live. Slowly, with the help of health professionals and medication, she clawed her way out of the depths.

In 2020, she decided to truly embrace her calling again and pursued certifications in coaching. She helps women who do not recognize themselves in the mirror as they have lost themselves in the roles of life.

Today she lives a life of purpose and continual healing. She is the proud mom of two teen boys and some spoiled pups.

# THE NAME IS LOVE ISLAND, SELF-LOVE ISLAND

By Stacey Short

"If you were put on an island tomorrow with no one else around, who would you be?" My therapist asked. At this point I had been in therapy for a few months. I came at the behest of my partner to try to save our failing relationship. I had two failed marriages under my belt already and could not IMAGINE failing at this relationship too, so I found myself every Wednesday on Cheryl's couch spilling my guts and trying to no longer drown in my life.

I looked at her like she had three heads. "What about the kids? What about my parents and my brothers, Geoff and Dan? How can I be on an island and not worry about them?" I was anxious and indignant. Who can just BE on an island and worry about WHO they are? What ridiculous exercise is this? All these thoughts were flooding my brain, almost short-circuiting it. "I'm a mom, sister, daughter, friend, employee, ex-wife, and current girlfriend."

"No, those are all ROLE you play. They are not WHO you are. They are in relation to others. On this island, the others don't exist. WHO are YOU?" I struggled with this answer. Tears started to well. I wanted to perform for her; I needed the right answer here, but it escaped me. "I don't understand what you're asking." I squeaked out through a tight throat. I genuinely could not tell her who I was outside of my roles or labels. I had been living in codependency and people-pleasing for so long I had NO idea who I was outside of anyone else. I left crying that day and many therapy days after that. The realization that I had been living my life for everyone BUT me hit me again and again. Those gut punches were brutal but needed.

It took me months to be able to answer that question. I had been raising two boys that were two years apart, on my second marriage, and my oldest son had been diagnosed with a primary immune deficiency, and I had almost lost him twice in the years before starting therapy. I gave up on my dreams of becoming a therapist and worked in hospitality for years. I needed the flexibility of being able to leave at the drop of a hat in case Bryce needed to be attended to. You can't do that as a family advocate for child sexual abuse. My ex-husband felt incapable of attending to Bryce alone because Bryce's case was complicated and could take a nasty turn with very little notice. The number of days and nights we have spent in a clinic, ER, or hospital is incalculable. I LIVED in crisis mode, just waiting for the other shoe to drop with him.

Life with Bryce started with me leaving an abusive and short-lived marriage eight months pregnant with him. The next few years were spent in specialists' offices, labs, rehabs, and many more medical offices. The longest stay in a hospital consecutively was 19 days as he had not only contracted C-Diff from being on antibiotics so much, but he had picked up Pseudomonas pneumonia from a prior hospital visit. He was 22 months old before an immunologist tested Bryce for a primary immune deficiency. We finally had a diagnosis and a course of treatment. That was only the tip of the iceberg. The long road to raising him was arduous, complicated, frustrating, and beautiful. In those 22 short months, I almost lost him twice due to his enigmatic health. He was a happy toddler full of love. I ended up pregnant with his brother, and he had a built-in best friend two years and two weeks after he came into this world.

I explain all this to show how easy it is to identify with your roles in life. I did not have a life or identity outside of my children. My marriage was suffering because I had nothing left to give at the end of the day to my spouse, let alone myself. Our relationship started to feel strained, and the opposing work hours left little time to be together as a couple. I didn't feel supported, heard, seen, or appreciated. I spent my days in doctors', therapists', or other offices. I spent hours monthly fighting insurance companies for life-saving medicine and interventions, teaching schools about Bryce, and advocating for his health. I spent the afternoons and nights at work 40 plus hours a week. I would come home to a quiet house five days a week. No one asked about my day, sat with me to eat dinner, or watched TV with me to unwind. Every night I was met with deafening silence. I would look around and think, "This can not be it. This can not be all there is to my life. There has to be more." I had no idea what I needed, but something inside me cried to be recognized.

I thought I was doing all the things right. I thought I was being a good wife, mother, daughter, employee, and friend. If you needed help moving, I was your girl. Need a shoulder to cry on? Pick me! I did everything for everyone around me and left nothing for myself at the end of the day. Boundaries were something I had heard about but never was allowed to set, nor was I taught. Saying no was unacceptable because I was being "rude" or "selfish." I was living a lonely existence in a house full of people. I needed help and wasn't getting the right kind at home, but I also did not know how to ask for the right kind.

So there I am, in 2014, being asked who I am on this lonely island. Attending these sessions was my first step towards self-care and, therefore, self-love. It took me months to answer it fully. My answer? I am a lover of music, learning, growing, animals, well-written books, water, travel, deep conversations, and life. How did I finally come to this answer? I got still. REALLY still.

My second act of self-love was to start attending yoga as many days a week as possible. I put on yoga clothes to take the kids to school, drop them off, and go to a yoga class that started in 15 minutes. I knew that if I wasn't under the gun with a start time, I'd go back home and get sucked into the couch again. I started slowly and built up eventually to

4-6 days a week for 90 minutes daily. I learned to listen to that inner voice that had been screaming. She wanted to be seen and cared for. I cried during savasana more times than I can remember. I knew I needed to return again and again, so I did.

Those glimmers of stillness grew and became contagious. I started to crave that stillness during the most hectic parts of my days. So, I started learning how to meditate. How to clear my mind as best as possible, batting the random thoughts away to focus on my breathing. I originally could not stop my mind chatter, so I set up a visualization to keep my mind active but quiet. I picture myself floating on a cool 80s type pool raft, hot pink, with flower pockets where the sun would heat the water to 'skin scalding.' I am floating on a black glass-like pool where I can feel the sun's warmth, but I am in a warm darkness. And I just float. Not in a creepy IT way, but in a "Wow! I can breathe" way.

The third way I implemented self-love was learning to breathe during difficult conversations. This breathing allowed me to think versus react. It allowed me to set boundaries, say no, and ask for a divorce. I stopped living my life for everyone else but me. It felt selfish. I was TOLD I was being selfish. I struggled not to internalize that and fall back into people-pleasing and codependent patterns. I got really fucking honest with myself, and that level of honesty is brutal. It requires a level of accountability that most of us avoid, whether we know that's what we're avoiding or not. I reached out for mental health help. I ended up on antidepressants for seven years. I am so glad I finally put myself first enough to make and keep doctors' appointments for me! When you take your young son to three doctors a week for his health, the LAST thing you want to do is go for yourself.

I find that story is so common with the women I have as clients. Yes, CLIENTS! In 2020, a friend told me about a health coach certification program she was looking into. She said it was actually health and life.

I heard my voice say, "I'll do it if you do it!" I never looked back or second-guessed my choice to pursue a career in coaching. I knew in my bones the minute I started the course that coaching was where I would find my soul's purpose. I never feel more in touch with myself than when I'm helping another woman move toward a more self-love filled life! In their healing, I find more healing for me. It's a beautiful synergy that I am honored to be a part of!

Healing is not linear, but it is continuous. Every day there is something to explore, get curious about, and possibly do differently. Start with one act of self-love and add on from there when you feel you have the capacity or when the first act feels like it's a part of your day easily. Look at yourself in the mirror, say no, and make and keep appointments for yourself. You are so worth caring for.

## Cheryl Leblanc

Widowed at the age of 37, a complete stranger to herself and uncertain of the future ahead Cheryl began her journey of self-exploration opening the door to the most profound lesson to be learned in this lifetime, the lesson of self-love.

It has been six years of self-exploration since her daughter's father passed and only now is she ready to begin sharing her love story with the world and mentoring others in the direction of self-love by embracing and harnessing the power of their vulnerability.

Newly navigating the world as an entrepreneur, mentor, coach and author Cheryl draws her motivation from her passion to create balance, love and tenderness in the world. The children of today require the best darn shot at an amazing future and that begins with us. By supporting one another and seeking the guidance of a mentor we can lead and guide the next generation through the chaos of life with self-love as our anchor and our compass.

# IF I DON'T HATE MYSELF, I MUST LOVE MYSELF, RIGHT?

## By Cheryl Leblanc

There comes a time in most people's lives that we begin to question why life is so difficult. Why am I sick and tired, and why do we have so much judgment and division in this world? For most of us, we arrive at these pivotal questions at a very difficult time in our life. Those difficult times often include divorce, death of a loved one, retirement, illness, or near-death experiences. This is a time of transition, where the old you begins to be unrecognizable, and the newest best version of yourself is preparing to be birthed forward. This transition does not have to come after or because of a difficult time; it can be a choice. You can choose to be the best version of yourself every day, and that starts with caring for yourself first and foremost. If you find yourself reading my words, I am here to tell you that you are being divinely guided to begin your journey of self-love. That pivotal moment has arrived without the pain to influence it.

The world we live in is so heavily divided by nationality, skin color, religion, political preference, gender, sexual preference, and the list goes on. All of these things create judgment and division among the people, and that causes chaos. That chaos we see in the world begins with our relationship with ourselves and the judgment we begin to place upon our own existence. Forfeiting pieces of ourselves to forcibly fit into those divisive categories, yearning to be seen and belong somewhere. Perhaps the journey to healing the world starts with self-love. By forgiving ourselves for our shortcomings, accepting all the good and bad that has shaped us into who we are, and loving that person and not forfeiting pieces of her, we can begin to love that way in the world and inspire others to do the same.

If I don't hate myself, I must love myself, right?

That's what I thought for most of my life. In all honesty, no one had ever even discussed self-love with me until I was thirty-seven years old. Perhaps in conversation, friends and family may have tried to hint at something like self-love, but they themselves were not fully aware of the concept either because it had never been taught to them.

Shortly after my first husband passed in 2017, after many nights spent alone with myself, I realized I was living with a complete stranger: myself. I had been living with this stranger for over twenty years. I just never slowed down enough or got quiet enough to witness her. How did life get so far off course that I didn't know that woman staring back at me in the mirror? A woman I had judged very harshly, doubted, and disrespected. If I don't hate her, I must love her, right? I used to justify being judgemental and critical of others against how judgemental I was of myself. I can judge others however I want as long as I judge myself even worse. My relationship with myself had become the worst relationship I had. When I finally saw that stranger in the mirror looking back at me, judged unfairly, sad, lost, and uncertain, I knew she needed help.

Every night after I put my three-year-old daughter to bed, my laptop became my best friend and counselor. After days upon days of searching the internet and scrolling through social media for hours, I stumbled upon an advertisement for an Akashic records reading in some small-town Alberta. I didn't even know what an Akashic records reading was, but the kind blonde woman that appeared on my screen called out to me, and I booked an appointment for the following afternoon.

When I spontaneously booked that appointment in the middle of the night, I failed to check the map. That small town Alberta was over 90 minutes away, giving me just enough time to get there, stay for the reading, and rush home to pick my daughter up from daycare. That whole 90-minute reading is a blur. All I can recall are the last fifteen to twenty minutes starting with, "Do you have any questions?"

I felt so silly asking a question that should be quite simple, "Self-love, what does it look like, and where do I begin?" The idea of self-love seemed simple, but the implementation of it was completely foreign.

That kind blonde woman softly explained to me that as mother, daughter, wife, friend, sister, or employee, we put everyone else's needs and desires ahead of our own, and at the end of the day, we are exhausted and have nothing left to give ourselves. Thirty-seven years searching for that place to be seen was met with a stranger in those twenty minutes; she understood me!!! And she gave me the knowledge of how to rekindle that relationship with myself.

"You begin by making the choice to spend quality time with yourself. You do one more small thing today for yourselves than you did yesterday. You can put the kids to bed early and have a bath or wake up early to have a cup of coffee and watch the sunrise. You do whatever your heart is calling you to do. It may be as simple as snoozing an extra fifteen minutes because you need the rest."

I still couldn't fully grasp how being selfish is self-love. Sacrifice my daughter's time with mom so that I can have me time? That would be so selfish of me. I'm supposed to spend every waking moment with her, loving her, and playing with her, am I not? That's what makes a good parent, isn't it?

That kind blonde woman was so patient and understanding of my confusion. She further explained that putting your desires ahead of your children's needs would be selfish. When you put your needs ahead of your child's desires, you are loving you. And by doing so, you are a happier, more loving, and present mom to her tomorrow. The alternative is she gets the tired, cranky uncared-for version of you.

Ahh-haaaa!!!!! I was starting to understand. That same stranger I was living with and disrespecting was the same woman who was parenting my daughter. What kind of example was I setting? Is this the mom I wanted to be? That stranger I was letting raise my daughter needed some tender love and care, ASAP. And so, the journey of self-love began—hot candle-lit baths, a new gym membership, a new diet, meditation, contemplation, masturbation, acceptance, forgiveness, emotional stability, and all that took place with a whole lot of patience.

On that journey to self-love, I was also grieving the death of my husband. I cried and begged god every night to just help me feel alive again like I wasn't alone and the world had not forgotten about me. At some point, I received a private message from a fella in an online group who was the right balance of persistent and respectful. That someone miraculously appeared and became a respected mentor. He helped me navigate that journey of self-love by establishing boundaries for me and keeping me focused on forward momentum. He helped me challenge my belief systems and often loaned me his confidence when I lacked confidence in myself. After about a year, we parted ways. That fella remains a dear friend in my life today. I would have never thought to find a coach or mentor. It just showed up. The support and collaboration helped me see my blind spots, adjust, and gain momentum.

The journey of self-love taught me how to love myself so that I could show someone else how to love me. My journey of self-love didn't just teach me about how I needed to be loved, it taught me what unconditional, accepting, and forgiving love looks like and how to share a love like that with the world. When you can love all aspects of yourself with acceptance and forgiveness, you can love others the same way and birth forth that kind of love into the world. A world that is torn apart from the inside out—where our inner world, insecurities, fear of judgment, and inability to forgive ourselves contaminate our relationship with the outside world.

Why is this not taught in schools? This might be the most profound lesson to learn in this lifetime: How to love properly, purely, and unconditionally, starting with yourself first.

When I had reached a level of self-love and self-awareness, I booked a retreat in Costa Rica, a place my soul had been called to for many years. This trip to Costa Rica was divinely led, however it met with many hurdles challenging my commitment to myself at every step. I didn't have the money to pay in full, but I knew I needed to go, so I made payment arrangements. This was the next step in my self-love and self-exploration journey, traveling alone to a foreign country. As I went to check in, I realized I had booked the flight in my maiden name, which did not match any of my identification. I had faith that if I spoke to someone in person and explained the situation, everything would work out. So, I hurried to the airport 20ish hours in advance and kindly asked the desk agent for her assistance. After a quick phone call, she was able to make the change without any fees. Even she was astonished. The following day as I boarded that plane, my own voice spoke to me, a voice I was only newly acquainted with. "You are going to meet your next great love." I journaled about it and hoped it to be true, I had been alone and single for two years. I was highly disappointed when none of the retreat guests measured up as my "next great love." Then in walked the property manager, and I could feel his presence before I saw him with my eyes. It was as if he glowed. We spoke briefly on my last day in Costa Rica, exchanged numbers, and sent a few texts upon return to Canada. I had to return to Canada to work on my self-love journey for another two years before I would return to Costa Rica and claim that man as my next great love.

I was actively enrolled in the Canadian Armed Forces and had been in the military for over fifteen years. It was a job that required uniformity and very little authentic expression. No wonder I had grown so distant from that woman staring back at me in the mirror. I abandoned her somewhere between fifteen years old and basic training. I had to retrieve that piece of myself, love that piece of myself, and forgive myself for how I had gotten so lost in this life. Once I fully embraced my authenticity and learned how to love myself with a uniform on, there was no longer a need to hide behind a uniform and a rank.

I met a group of women who taught me how to dream again, that there was more this life had to offer than hoping for a promotion and moving out of military housing. I wrote down a series of dreams: leaving the military, starting a business, living part-time in Canada and Costa Rica or Bali, and falling in love. One year after I wrote down my dreams and shared them with the world, I retired from the military and was planning a move to Mexico with a friend. Something was stopping me from booking the tickets to Mexico besides my father's complete disapproval. My soul was hesitant. I knew I was meant to go to Costa Rica, but how could I move to a new country alone with a seven-year-old? In a wild leap of faith, I texted that property manager, hoping he could offer some assistance with the relocation. To my surprise, he still had the number and was welcoming, kind, and helpful. Less than 10 days after messaging him, in the midst of a pandemic, I booked two one-way tickets to Costa Rica. After settling in, our relationship shifted from assistance to friends, and before long, we were having a conversation with my daughter about getting married and being a family.

I cannot say the past year has been rainbows and butterflies. We have been challenged in so many ways. Different cultures, bad choices, finances, and a blended family, but the one thing that has not waivered one bit is Love. We are all human and flawed. We will make mistakes, and our insecurities and fears will steer us in the wrong direction at times, but love is our compass and love is our anchor. When we can show the outside world the same acceptance and forgiveness that we have shown ourselves, we begin to heal together. Being anchored in self-love has trumped my insecurities and fears so they don't trigger and lash out to hurt the people around me. I cannot say the past year is all my doing because love is a dance, sometimes we lead and sometimes we follow. What I do know for certain is God delivered me here to Costa Rica when I had mastered self-love so that I could lead when needed with unconditional, accepting, and forgiving love. That love has allowed me to be soft and tender, to create the space for my husband to lean in and be vulnerable without judgment, and begin to show my husband how to love and forgive himself. This kind of love does not stop at my husband. We share and demonstrate this kind of forgiving, encompassing love with our children, our families, and our communities.

More conversations, community, collaborations, and coaches are needed to spread the message of self-love far and wide into the world. We will not change the chaos in the world overnight, and probably not in this lifetime. What we can do is start to shift our inner world and embark on our own self-love journey. In doing so, we will influence our small little piece of the world and begin to be the change we wish to see in the world. We may live in a world full of division and chaos, but what we all have in common is that we are human, we are flawed, we make mistakes, and we all have insecurities and fears that cloud our vision of the present moment. Even those among us who appear to have life figured out, that we look to with admiration, have their flaws. There is not a human on this planet that can do this life alone. We are wired for community and connection. We need to be seen as we are and met with acceptance and forgiveness, and that all starts with self-love, accepting, and forgiving yourself first and foremost.

# JOIN THE MOVEMENT!
# #BAUW

## Becoming An Unstoppable Woman
## With She Rises Studios

She Rises Studios was founded by Hanna Olivas and Adriana Luna Carlos, the mother-daughter duo, in mid-2020 as they saw a need to help empower women around the world. They are the podcast hosts of the *She Rises Studios Podcast* as well as Amazon best-selling authors and motivational speakers who travel the world. Hanna and Adriana are the movement creators of #BAUW - Becoming An Unstoppable Woman: The movement has been created to universally impact women of all ages, at whatever stage of life, to overcome insecurities, and adversities, and develop an unstoppable mindset. She Rises Studios educates, celebrates, and empowers women globally.

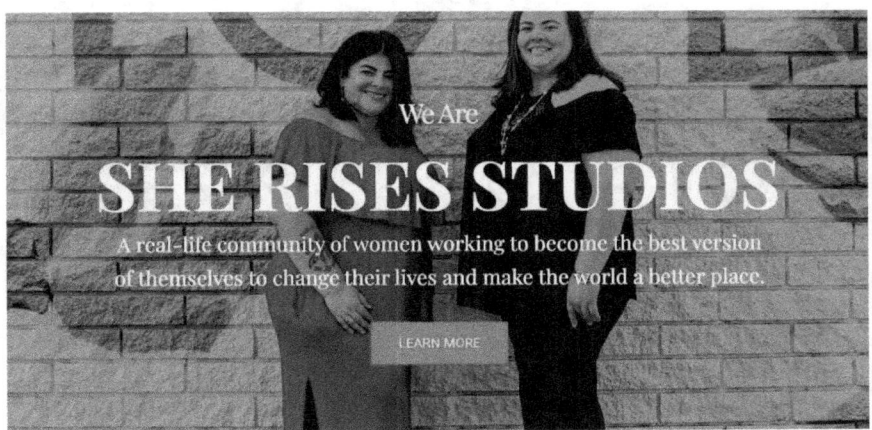

## Looking to Join Us in our Next Anthology or Publish YOUR Own?

She Rises Studios Publishing offers full-service publishing, marketing, book tour, and campaign services. For more information, contact info@sherisesstudios.com

We are always looking for women who want to share their stories and expertise and feature their businesses on our podcasts, in our books, and in our magazines.

## SEE WHAT WE DO

**OUR PODCAST**

**OUR BOOKS**

**OUR SERVICES**

Be featured in the Becoming An Unstoppable Woman magazine, published in 13 countries and sold in all major retailers. Get the visibility you need to LEVEL UP in your business!

Have your own TV show streamed across major platforms like Roku TV, Amazon Fire Stick, Apple TV and more!

Learn to leverage your expertise. Build your online presence and grow your audience with Fenix TV.
https://fenixtv.sherisesstudios.com/

Visit www.SheRisesStudios.com to see how YOU can join the #BAUW movement and help your community to achieve the UNSTOPPABLE mindset.

Have you checked out the *She Rises Studios Podcast?*

Find us on all MAJOR platforms: Spotify, IHeartRadio, Apple Podcasts, Google Podcasts, etc.

**Looking to become a sponsor or build a partnership?**

Email us at info@sherisesstudios.com